INTERVIEW QUESTIONS AND ANSWERS

COMPREHENSIVE GUIDE TO WIN JOBS

Dora Harris

TABLE OF CONTENTS

INTRODUCTION

5

CHAPTER ONE   **10**

WHAT IS INTERVIEW

10

CHAPTER TWO   **17**

UNLOCKING THE GATEWAY TO SUCCESS 17

CHAPTER THREE

24

EFFECTIVE INTERVIEW COMMUNICATION
GUIDE   24

Verbal Communication: 24

Non-Verbal Communication   26

Dressing for Success   27

Timing   27

Additional Tips

28

CHAPTER FOUR   31

RESEARCH BEFORE JOB INTERVIEW

31

CHAPTER FIVE   **38**

152 COMMON INTERVIEW QUESTIONS AND
ANSWERS

38

CHAPTER SIX   109

UNDERSTANDING THE INTERVIEWER'S
CONCERNS   109

CHAPTER SEVEN **113**

    CONCLUSION

                113

LETTER TO MY READERS **118**

INTRODUCTION

In the intricate dance of the professional world, where opportunities and challenges intermingle, the concept of "Interview Questions and Answers" stands as a pivotal gateway.

Interviews, with their structured inquiries and thoughtful responses, serve as the linchpin in various spheres of life, shaping destinies and influencing trajectories. As individuals navigate the labyrinth of job searches, journalistic pursuits, or academic investigations, the exchange of questions and answers emerges as a crucial medium for understanding, evaluation, and connection.

At the heart of this phenomenon lies the art of crafting questions that serve as portals into the depth and breadth of a candidate's abilities, experiences, and character. Whether posed by a hiring manager seeking the perfect fit for a job role, a journalist unraveling the layers of a story, or a researcher exploring the nuances of human experiences, the questions laid out become instruments of discovery and discernment. For job seekers, the journey through interviews is akin to a high-stakes odyssey.

The questions posed by potential employers are not merely interrogative; they are strategic probes delving into a candidate's skills, knowledge, and cultural compatibility. The anticipation of facing inquiries about strengths, weaknesses, and career aspirations prompts individuals to embark on meticulous self-reflection and preparation.

It is in the thoughtful articulation of responses that candidates endeavor to present themselves as not just suitable but exceptional contenders for the coveted role. Conversely, for employers, the formulation of interview questions requires a delicate balance between insight and fairness. Each question is a calibrated instrument, aimed at extracting information that transcends the confines of a resume. Employers seek to uncover not only the technical prowess of a candidate but also their problem-solving acumen, adaptability, and interpersonal skills. The spectrum of questions may span behavioral queries that illuminate past actions and decisions to situational scenarios that test a candidate's ability to navigate challenges in real-time.

In the realm of journalism, interviews serve as the lifeblood of storytelling. Journalists, armed with curiosity and a thirst for truth, deploy questions as tools to unravel narratives, validate facts, and capture the essence of events.

The questions asked in an interview can shape the trajectory of a story, revealing insights that go beyond the surface and breathe life into the reporting. The art of questioning becomes a dynamic dance between the interviewer and interviewee, each step revealing new layers of information and perspective.

In academic and research pursuits, interviews are integral to the qualitative exploration of human experiences and phenomena. Researchers craft questions that open windows into the thoughts, emotions, and motivations of participants. These inquiries, often framed with precision and sensitivity, seek to uncover patterns, generate understanding, and contribute to the broader body of knowledge in a particular field.

As we embark on this exploration of "Interview Questions and Answers," we delve into a realm where words become the currency of exchange, ideas are tested, and destinies are shaped.

This topic encapsulates the art and science of human interaction, where the right question, posed at the right moment, can unravel layers of complexity, reveal hidden potentials, and forge connections that transcend the confines of the interview room. It is a journey into the heart of communication, where questions and answers become threads weaving the intricate tapestry of personal and professional narratives.

CHAPTER ONE

WHAT IS INTERVIEW

An interview is a structured conversation between two or more individuals with a specific purpose, commonly used in various contexts such as employment, journalism, research, and information gathering.

This dynamic exchange serves as a platform for one party, often the interviewer, to pose questions and the other, the interviewee, to respond, sharing information, insights, or opinions.

In the realm of employment, job interviews are a crucial component of the hiring process. Employers use interviews to evaluate a candidate's qualifications, skills, and suitability for a particular role. These interactions allow hiring managers to delve beyond the information presented on a resume, gaining a more comprehensive understanding of the candidate's personality, communication abilities, and potential cultural fit within the organization.

Journalistic interviews are conducted by reporters to gather information, verify facts, and obtain firsthand accounts of events or experiences. These interviews are often conducted with experts, eyewitnesses, or individuals directly involved in a story.

Journalists employ various interview styles, ranging from structured and formal to informal and conversational, depending on the nature of the story and the desired information.

Research interviews play a fundamental role in academic and scientific investigations. Researchers employ interviews to collect data, gather perspectives, and gain deeper insights into a particular subject. Whether conducted in person, over the phone, or through video conferencing, these interviews provide a qualitative approach to understanding complex phenomena and human experiences.

The structure of an interview can vary widely based on its purpose and the nature of the interaction. Some interviews follow a rigid format, with predetermined questions and a standardized approach. Others adopt a more conversational style, allowing for flexibility and spontaneity in the exchange. Regardless of the format, effective interviews require careful planning, active listening, and thoughtful questioning.

Preparation is a key element in ensuring a successful interview, particularly for job seekers. Candidates are encouraged to research the company, understand the job requirements, and anticipate common interview questions. Employers, on the other hand, must carefully craft questions that assess a candidate's skills, experience, and cultural fit within the organization.

During an interview, effective communication skills are paramount. Both the interviewer and interviewee must articulate their thoughts clearly, express themselves concisely, and actively engage in the conversation. Non-verbal cues, such as body language and facial expressions, also play a significant role in conveying information and understanding the nuances of the exchange.

The interview process extends beyond the verbal interaction itself. Post-interview, employers may conduct follow-up assessments, reference checks, and additional evaluations to make informed hiring decisions. Candidates, on the other hand, may send thank-you notes expressing gratitude and reiterating their interest in the position.

An interview serves as a dynamic and multifaceted tool with applications across diverse fields. It facilitates the exchange of information, the evaluation of qualifications, and the exploration of perspectives. Whether in the context of employment, journalism, or research, interviews are a fundamental mechanism for gathering insights, making informed decisions, and building meaningful connections.

Effective interviewing requires careful preparation, active communication, and a thoughtful approach to extracting valuable information from the participants involved.

CHAPTER TWO

UNLOCKING THE GATEWAY TO SUCCESS

In the dynamic landscape of professional growth, the job interview stands as a crucial juncture where aspirations meet reality. The art of acing an interview lies not just in a polished resume but also in the ability to navigate a labyrinth of questions and deliver impactful answers.

This pivotal interaction between a candidate and an employer is the make-or-break moment that can shape careers and reshape destinies. Thus, delving into the intricacies of interview questions and answers becomes imperative for those striving for career advancement and fulfillment.

The Power of Questions: Interviews are a multifaceted process designed to unearth a candidate's suitability for a role beyond the confines of a CV. Questions become the medium through which an employer peels away layers to reveal the essence of a candidate's skills, experiences, and character.

They serve as a window into the candidate's thought processes, problem-solving abilities, and cultural fit within an organization. From the classic "Tell me about yourself" to the more nuanced behavioral questions, each query is a strategic tool aimed at understanding the depth and breadth of a candidate's professional acumen.

The Science of Answers: Crafting responses that resonate positively is an art form that requires a combination of self-awareness, preparation, and effective communication skills. The candidate must not only showcase their qualifications but also align their narrative with the organization's values and objectives.

A well-crafted answer transcends a mere recounting of experiences; it serves as a vehicle for demonstrating one's ability to learn, adapt, and contribute to the prospective workplace. Beyond technical proficiency, employers seek individuals with the capacity for critical thinking, collaboration, and innovation—all of which can be communicated through thoughtful responses.

Navigating Common Ground: Interviews often traverse a common terrain of questions that touch upon strengths, weaknesses, challenges, and achievements. Understanding the underlying motivations behind these questions can empower candidates to tailor their answers strategically.

What might seem like a probing inquiry into weaknesses is, in reality, an opportunity to showcase self-awareness and growth. Similarly, discussing achievements provides a platform to highlight skills, resilience, and the ability to deliver tangible results. By decoding the purpose behind these questions, candidates can transform the interview into a collaborative dialogue rather than a mere interrogation.

Beyond the Traditional: In the contemporary job market, interviews have evolved beyond traditional formats. Competency-based interviews, situational judgment tests, and behavioral assessments are becoming increasingly prevalent. This shift underscores the importance of not just rote memorization of answers but the development of a versatile skill set that can adapt to diverse interview methodologies.

Navigating these variations requires candidates to not only understand industry-specific expectations but also to cultivate an agility that allows them to showcase their strengths in varied contexts.

Continuous Learning and Adaptation: The landscape of interview questions and answers is ever-evolving, mirroring the dynamic nature of industries and workplaces. As technology advances, and organizational structures transform, candidates must stay attuned to emerging trends in interview practices.

Continuous learning, not only in terms of technical skills but also in the realm of interpersonal and communication skills, becomes a cornerstone for success in navigating the evolving interview landscape.

In this exploration of interview questions and answers, we embark on a journey to unravel the layers of this intricate dance between employers and candidates. As we delve into the nuances of responses, decode the intentions behind questions, and adapt to the changing landscapes of interviews, we equip ourselves with the tools to unlock the gateway to success.

In the realm of professional aspirations, the ability to articulate one's story and skills is not just a prerequisite; it is the key that opens doors to new opportunities and paves the way for a fulfilling career journey.

CHAPTER THREE

EFFECTIVE INTERVIEW COMMUNICATION GUIDE

Speaking to an interviewer effectively involves a combination of verbal communication, non-verbal cues, and professional etiquette. Here's a comprehensive guide on how to speak to an interviewer:

Verbal Communication:

Research and Preparation: Before going for an interview, do a brief research about the company and the role you're applying for.Prepare answers to common interview questions.Always familiarize yourself with your resume or CV and be ready to discuss your experiences without stammering.

Clarity and Conciseness: Speak clearly and at a moderate pace.Avoid using excessive jargon; explain technical terms when necessary. Be concise in your responses, focusing on key points.

Positive Tone: Try to maintain a positive and enthusiastic tone throughout the interview. Always express your interest in the position and the company you applied for.

Active Listening: Pay close attention to the interviewer's questions. Pause before responding to ensure you've fully understood the question. Demonstrate active listening by nodding and providing appropriate verbal cues.

Ask Questions: Prepare thoughtful questions to ask the interviewer. This will go a long way to demonstrate your genuine interest in the position and the company.

Non-Verbal Communication

Body Language:Maintain good posture to convey confidence. Make eye contact, but don't stare. Use gestures naturally and sparingly.

Facial Expressions:Smile appropriately to convey friendliness. Avoid excessive frowning or other negative expressions.

Handshake:Offer a firm and confident handshake. Ensure your hands are dry and free of distractions like excessive jewelry.

Dressing for Success

Professional Attire: Make your research and choose clothing that is appropriate for the company culture. Wear a suit or business attire that is clean and well-fitted.

Grooming: Ensure your hair is clean and well-groomed. Keep accessories and makeup (if applicable) conservative.

Footwear: Choose polished and appropriate shoes that match your outfit.

Timing

Punctuality: Aim to arrive 10-15 minutes early for the interview. Late arrival may give a negative impression.

Scheduling: If given options for interview times, choose a time when you're most alert and focused.

Avoid Rush Hour: Schedule your interview to avoid rush hour if possible.
This helps reduce the stress of potential delays.

Day of the Week: Tuesday to Thursday is often considered the best time for interviews.

Additional Tips

Politeness: Use polite language and address the interviewer by their title and last name unless instructed otherwise.

Follow-Up: Send a thank-you email after the interview expressing your appreciation for the opportunity.

Adaptability: Be prepared to adapt to different interview formats, such as one-on-one, panel, or behavioral interviews.

By combining effective verbal communication, positive non-verbal cues, and professional presentation, you increase your chances of leaving a lasting positive impression on the interviewer.

CHAPTER FOUR

RESEARCH BEFORE JOB INTERVIEW

Researching your potential place of work before going for an interview is a crucial step in ensuring a successful and fulfilling career. This proactive approach not only demonstrates your genuine interest in the company but also provides you with valuable insights that can significantly impact your decision-making process. Here are some key reasons why making research about your potential place of work is important.

Company Culture: Understanding the company culture is essential for determining whether you will thrive in that environment. Researching the organization's values, mission, and work culture can help you assess whether your own values align with those of the company. This information is vital for long-term job satisfaction and overall career success.

Job Expectations: Thorough research allows you to gain clarity on the specific requirements and expectations of the job you're applying for. Knowing the responsibilities, skills needed, and potential challenges will help you tailor your responses during the interview, demonstrating that you are well-prepared and have a genuine interest in the role.

Industry Knowledge: Being well-informed about the industry in which the company operates showcases your dedication and professionalism. Employers appreciate candidates who have a good understanding of the industry trends, competitors, and challenges. This knowledge allows you to engage in meaningful conversations during the interview, showcasing your enthusiasm for the industry.

Company Performance: Researching the financial stability and performance of the company provides you with an understanding of its overall health. This information can influence your decision to accept an offer, as it helps you assess the company's long-term viability and potential for growth.

Team and Leadership: Knowing about the key players in the company, including the leadership team, can give you valuable insights into the organizational structure. It allows you to understand the management style and the dynamics of the team you might be working with, helping you determine whether it's a good fit for your working style and career goals.

Recent News and Developments: Staying up-to-date with the company's recent news, achievements, and challenges positions you as an informed candidate. It also provides you with relevant topics to discuss during the interview, demonstrating that you are engaged and interested in the company's current affairs.

Now, on the importance of not missing the interview.

Professionalism: Missing an interview is unprofessional and can damage your reputation in the industry. It reflects poorly on your commitment and reliability, traits that are highly valued by employers.

Missed Opportunities: Interviews are not just an opportunity for the employer to evaluate you; they are also a chance for you to assess whether the company aligns with your career goals. Missing an interview means missing the chance to explore potential opportunities and make an informed decision about your future.

First Impressions Matter: An interview is often the first direct interaction with a potential employer. Missing it sends a negative message about your level of interest and dedication, which can impact your chances of being considered for the position.

Conducting thorough research before an interview demonstrates your commitment and allows you to make an informed decision about your potential place of work. Additionally, not missing the interview is crucial for maintaining professionalism, seizing opportunities, and making a positive first impression on your prospective employer.

CHAPTER FIVE

152 COMMON INTERVIEW QUESTIONS AND ANSWERS

1. TELL ME ABOUT YOURSELF.

ANSWER: Provide a brief overview of your professional background, highlighting relevant experience and skills. Focus on aspects that align with the job you're interviewing for.

2. WHAT ARE YOUR STRENGTHS AND WEAKNESSES?

ANSWER: For strengths, discuss skills directly related to the job. For weaknesses, choose a genuine weakness but emphasize how you've worked to improve or manage it.

3. WHAT IS YOUR PREFERRED
    WORK STYLE?

ANSWER: Tailor your response to the company culture. Discuss your adaptability, ability to work independently or in a team, and any relevant work style preferences.

4. HOW DO YOU STAY UPDATED
    ON INDUSTRY TRENDS AND
    DEVELOPMENTS?

ANSWER: Discuss specific sources you use, such as industry publications, conferences, or online forums. Emphasize your commitment to staying current in your field.

5. DO YOU HAVE ANY QUESTIONS
    FOR US?

ANSWER: Always have questions prepared. Inquire about company culture, team dynamics, or specific details about the role. It shows your genuine interest and engagement.

6. HOW DO YOU HANDLE STRESS AND PRESSURE?

ANSWER: Provide examples of situations where you manage stress effectively and achieve positive outcomes.

7. WHY SHOULD WE HIRE YOU?

ANSWER: Highlight your unique skills, experiences, and how they make you the ideal candidate for the job.

8. DESCRIBE A SITUATION WHERE YOU HAD TO MEET A TIGHT DEADLINE.

ANSWER: Emphasize your time-management and prioritization skills, and the successful outcome.

9. WHAT MOTIVATES YOU?

ANSWER:Discuss intrinsic and extrinsic motivators, linking them to the job you're applying for.

10. HOW DO YOU HANDLE CONSTRUCTIVE CRITICISM?

ANSWER: Show openness to feedback and provide an example of how you used it to improve.

11. DESCRIBE A SITUATION WHERE YOU HAD TO WORK ON A PROJECT WITH TIGHT RESOURCES.

ANSWER: Highlight your resourcefulness, creativity, and ability to achieve results with limited resources.

12. WHAT DO YOU KNOW ABOUT OUR COMPETITORS?

ANSWER: Research the company's main competitors and briefly discuss their strengths and weaknesses.

13. HOW DO YOU CONTRIBUTE TO FOSTERING A POSITIVE WORK ENVIRONMENT?

ANSWER: Mention your communication skills, teamwork, and any initiatives you've taken to promote a positive atmosphere.

14. CAN YOU PROVIDE AN EXAMPLE OF WHEN YOU HAD TO DEAL WITH A DIFFICULT TEAM MEMBER?

ANSWER: Highlight your conflict resolution skills and ability to work collaboratively even in challenging situations.

15. WHAT DO YOU THINK IS THE BIGGEST CHALLENGE OUR INDUSTRY IS FACING?

ANSWER: Demonstrate your industry knowledge and offer thoughtful insights into current challenges.

16. HOW DO YOU KEEP YOUR TECHNICAL SKILLS CURRENT?

ANSWER: Discuss any ongoing training, certifications, or personal projects that keep your skills up-to-date.

17. TELL ME ABOUT A TIME WHEN YOU HAD TO LEAD A TEAM.

ANSWER: Use the STAR method to describe the situation, your role, actions taken, and the positive outcome.

18. WHAT INTERESTS YOU ABOUT OUR PRODUCTS/SERVICES?

ANSWER: Showcase your knowledge of the company's offerings and how your skills align with contributing to their success.

19.HOW WOULD YOU HANDLE
TIGHT DEADLINES AND
MULTIPLE PROJECTS AT SAME
TIME?

ANSWER: Describe your organizational
skills, time-management strategies, and
ability to remain focused under pressure.

20.WHY DO YOU WANT THIS JOB?

ANSWER: Discuss how the job aligns with
your skills, career goals, and values.
Mention specific aspects of the company or
role that is appealing to you.

21.WHERE DO YOU SEE YOURSELF
IN 5 YEARS?

ANSWER: Express your ambition and
desire for growth, emphasizing how you see
yourself contributing to the company's
success.

22. WHY SHOULD WE HIRE YOU?

ANSWER: Highlight your unique skills, experiences, and achievements that make you the best fit for the position.

23. WHAT DO YOU KNOW ABOUT OUR COMPANY?

ANSWER: Demonstrate your research by mentioning key facts about the company, its values, and recent achievements.

24. WHAT IS YOUR GREATEST PROFESSIONAL ACHIEVEMENT?

ANSWER: Share a specific accomplishment, emphasizing your contributions and the positive impact on the team or company.

25. WHAT ARE YOUR SALARY EXPECTATIONS?

ANSWER: Provide a salary range based on industry standards and your research on the company's compensation practices.

26. HOW DO YOU HANDLE FEEDBACK?

ANSWER: Express your openness to feedback, your ability to learn from it, and provide an example of a situation where you improved based on feedback.

27. WHAT MOTIVATES YOU?

Answer: Discuss intrinsic and extrinsic motivators, emphasizing how they align with the role and contribute to your job satisfaction.

28. HOW DO YOU HANDLE TIGHT DEADLINES?

ANSWER: Describe your approach to managing deadlines, including prioritization, effective planning, and staying focused under pressure.

29. WHAT DO YOU CONSIDER YOUR TECHNICAL STRENGTHS?

ANSWER: Highlight your technical skills relevant to the job, providing examples of how you've applied them in previous roles.

30. HOW DO YOU HANDLE CONFLICT IN A TEAM?

ANSWER: Discuss your approach to conflict resolution, emphasizing communication, collaboration, and finding common ground.

31. HOW DO YOU HANDLE COMPETING PRIORITIES?

ANSWER: Discuss your method for assessing priorities, organizing tasks, and ensuring that all essential tasks are completed on time.

32. TELL ME ABOUT A TIME WHEN YOU FAILED. HOW DID YOU HANDLE IT?

ANSWER: Discuss a specific failure, what you learned from it, and how you applied those lessons to future situations.

33. HOW DO YOU ENSURE ATTENTION TO DETAIL IN YOUR WORK?

ANSWER: Describe your methods for double-checking work, creating checklists, and being thorough to avoid mistakes.

34. CAN YOU DESCRIBE A SITUATION WHERE YOU HAD TO WORK WITH A DIFFICULT TEAM MEMBER?

ANSWER: Detail the situation, your approach to collaboration, and how you contributed to resolving conflicts and achieving team goals.

35. HOW DO YOU HANDLE TIGHT BUDGETS OR RESOURCE CONSTRAINTS?

ANSWER: Discuss your experience with resource management, cost-cutting strategies, and finding creative solutions to achieve goals within constraints.

36. WHAT DO YOU THINK MAKES A GREAT LEADER?

ANSWER: Outline qualities such as communication, empathy, decisiveness, and the ability to inspire others, providing examples of how you embody these traits.

37. CAN YOU PROVIDE AN EXAMPLE OF A TIME WHEN YOU HAD TO MEET A CHALLENGING GOAL?

ANSWER: Use the SMART criteria (Specific, Measurable, Achievable, Relevant, Time-bound) to describe the goal and how you successfully achieved it.

38. WHAT STRATEGIES DO YOU USE TO STAY ORGANIZED?

ANSWER: Discuss tools, systems, or personal habits you use to stay organized, ensuring you can manage multiple tasks efficiently.

39. HOW DO YOU HANDLE A SITUATION WHERE YOU HAVE TO DELEGATE TASKS?

ANSWER: Explain your approach to delegation, including how you assess team members' strengths and allocate tasks accordingly, while providing necessary support.

40. HOW DO YOU KEEP YOUR SKILLS UP-TO-DATE IN A

RAPIDLY CHANGING
INDUSTRY?

ANSWER: Discuss your commitment to
continuous learning, mentioning courses,
certifications, or other methods you use to
stay current in your field.

41.HOW DO YOU HANDLE
SITUATIONS WHERE YOU
DISAGREE WITH YOUR
SUPERVISOR OR TEAM
MEMBER?

ANSWER: "I believe in open
communication and constructive dialogue.
In situations of disagreement, I express my
perspective respectfully, actively listen to
others' viewpoints, and work towards
finding a solution that aligns with the team's
goals."

42. PROJECT IS NOT GOING AS
PLANNED?

ANSWER: "In such situations, I assess the challenges, identify root causes, and collaborate with the team to develop a revised plan. I believe in being proactive, seeking input from team members, and making necessary adjustments to get the project back on track."

43. HOW DO YOU CONTRIBUTE TO FOSTERING A POSITIVE WORK ENVIRONMENT?

ANSWER: "I contribute to a positive work environment by being approachable, actively listening to colleagues, and promoting open communication. I believe in recognizing and celebrating achievements

44. WHAT TECHNICAL SKILLS DO YOU POSSESS THAT MAKE YOU WELL-SUITED FOR THIS ROLE?

ANSWER: "I have strong proficiency in [mention specific technical skills relevant to the job, e.g., programming languages, software, or tools]. These skills have been honed through [X years] of practical experience in [related projects or roles]."

45. CAN YOU PROVIDE EXAMPLES OF YOUR EXPERIENCE WITH PROJECT MANAGEMENT AND COORDINATION?

ANSWER: "In my previous role, I led [mention a specific project] from initiation to completion. I demonstrated strong project management skills by defining milestones, coordinating team efforts, and ensuring the project was delivered on time and within scope."

46. WHAT PROGRAMMING LANGUAGES ARE YOU PROFICIENT IN, AND HOW HAVE YOU APPLIED THEM IN YOUR PREVIOUS ROLES?

ANSWER: "I am proficient in [mention programming languages, e.g., Python, Java] and have applied them extensively in tasks such as [mention specific projects or tasks where these languages were utilized]. These skills have proven essential in optimizing processes and improving efficiency."

47. DESCRIBE YOUR EXPERIENCE WITH DATA VISUALIZATION TOOLS AND TECHNIQUES.

Answer: "I have experience using data visualization tools like [mention specific tools, e.g., Tableau]. In a previous role, I created visualizations that effectively communicated complex data insights to both technical and non-technical stakeholders, facilitating informed decision-making."

48. HOW DO YOU APPROACH COLLABORATING WITH CROSS-FUNCTIONAL TEAMS?

ANSWER: "I believe in open communication and collaboration. In my previous roles, I actively engaged with cross-functional teams by facilitating regular meetings, sharing progress updates, and ensuring everyone was aligned towards common goals."

49. DISCUSS YOUR EXPERIENCE IN DEVELOPING AND IMPLEMENTING SUCCESSFUL MARKETING STRATEGIES.

ANSWER: "I have a proven track record in developing and implementing marketing strategies that have led to [mention specific achievements, e.g., increased brand visibility or revenue growth]. My approach involves a thorough understanding of the target audience and leveraging data-driven insights."

50. WHAT EXPERIENCE DO YOU HAVE WITH CUSTOMER RELATIONSHIP MANAGEMENT (CRM) SOFTWARE?

ANSWER: "I am proficient in using CRM software such as [mention specific CRM software]. In my previous roles, I effectively utilized CRM tools to manage customer relationships, track interactions, and analyze data to enhance customer satisfaction and retention."

51. DISCUSS YOUR EXPERIENCE WITH BUDGET MANAGEMENT AND FINANCIAL ANALYSIS.

ANSWER: "I have a strong background in budget management and financial analysis. In my previous role, I was responsible for [mention specific financial responsibilities], where I successfully [mention specific achievements, e.g., cost savings or improved financial efficiency]."

52. HOW DO YOU APPROACH USER EXPERIENCE (UX) DESIGN, AND CAN YOU PROVIDE EXAMPLES OF PROJECTS WHERE YOU APPLIED UX PRINCIPLES?

ANSWER: "I approach UX design by focusing on user needs and creating intuitive, user-friendly interfaces. In a recent project, I applied UX principles to [mention specific project details], resulting in [mention positive outcomes, e.g., improved user engagement or satisfaction]."

53. DESCRIBE YOUR EXPERIENCE IN DEVELOPING AND IMPLEMENTING CYBERSECURITY MEASURES.

ANSWER: "I have a comprehensive background in developing and implementing cybersecurity measures to protect against threats. In my previous role, I played a key role in [mention specific cybersecurity initiatives], resulting in enhanced system security and data protection."

54. HOW DO YOU APPROACH DATA PRIVACY AND COMPLIANCE IN YOUR WORK?

ANSWER: "I prioritize data privacy and compliance by staying informed about relevant regulations, such as [mention specific regulations, e.g., GDPR]. In my previous roles, I implemented measures to ensure data integrity and compliance, conducting regular audits and updates."

55. DESCRIBE YOUR EXPERIENCE WITH NETWORK INFRASTRUCTURE AND TROUBLESHOOTING.

ANSWER: "I have hands-on experience with network infrastructure and troubleshooting. In my previous roles, I managed [mention specific aspects, e.g., network configurations, security protocols] and resolved issues promptly to ensure uninterrupted operations."

56. HOW DO YOU APPROACH COLLABORATION WITH UX/UI DESIGNERS IN THE DEVELOPMENT PROCESS?

ANSWER: "I believe in close collaboration with UX/UI designers to ensure a seamless integration of design and functionality. In past projects, I actively engaged with designers to understand user experience goals and implemented technical solutions that aligned with the design vision."

57. DESCRIBE A SITUATION WHERE YOU HAD TO DEAL WITH A DIFFICULT TEAM MEMBER. HOW DID YOU HANDLE IT?

ANSWER: I once had a team member who was resistant to change. I initiated an open conversation to understand their concerns, addressed their issues, and worked together to find common ground. This approach helped improve teamwork and productivity.

58. CAN YOU SHARE AN EXAMPLE OF A CHALLENGE YOU FACED IN A PREVIOUS JOB AND HOW YOU OVERCAME IT?

ANSWER: In a previous role, we faced a sudden change in project requirements. I gathered the team, brainstormed solutions, and implemented a flexible plan that accommodated the changes. This adaptability resulted in a successful project completion.

59. HOW DID YOU MOTIVATE YOUR TEAM?

ANSWER: I took the lead on a complex project by setting clear goals, providing support, and recognizing individual contributions. Regular check-ins and positive reinforcement created a motivated and collaborative team environment.

60. HOW DID YOU ADDRESS THEIR CONCERNS?

ANSWER: I once had a client who was unhappy with the deliverables. I actively listened to their concerns, acknowledged the issues, and presented a revised plan. By demonstrating responsiveness and commitment to their satisfaction, we were able to salvage the relationship.

61. CAN YOU SHARE AN EXAMPLE OF A TIME WHEN YOU HAD TO ADAPT TO A SIGNIFICANT CHANGE IN THE WORKPLACE?

ANSWER: In a previous job, there was a major organizational restructuring. I adapted by staying informed, being flexible, and proactively seeking opportunities within the new structure. This allowed me to contribute positively to the evolving work environment.

62. HOW DID YOU APPROACH IT?

ANSWER: I identified the root cause of the conflict, organized a team meeting to address concerns, and facilitated an open dialogue. By promoting understanding and compromise, we resolved the conflict and strengthened team dynamics.

63. DESCRIBE A TIME WHEN YOU HAD TO LEARN A NEW SKILL QUICKLY TO MEET JOB REQUIREMENTS.

ANSWER: In a previous role, I needed to learn a new software tool. I took the initiative to attend training sessions, practiced consistently, and sought guidance from experts. Within a short period, I became proficient in the tool and contributed effectively to projects.

64. CAN YOU SHARE AN EXAMPLE OF A SUCCESSFUL PROJECT YOU WORKED ON? WHAT WAS YOUR ROLE, AND HOW DID

YOU CONTRIBUTE TO ITS
SUCCESS?

ANSWER: In my last position, I played a
key role in a project that increased efficiency
by implementing process improvements. My
responsibilities included analyzing current
workflows, proposing changes, and leading
the team through successful implementation,
resulting in a 20% improvement in
productivity.

65.HOW DID YOU NAVIGATE
THROUGH UNCERTAINTIES?

ANSWER: I encountered ambiguity in a
project due to changing client requirements.
I initiated regular communication with the
client to clarify expectations, set realistic
milestones, and established a feedback loop.
This proactive approach helped us navigate
uncertainties and deliver a successful
project.

66. CAN YOU SHARE AN EXAMPLE OF A TIME WHEN YOU HAD TO COLLABORATE WITH COLLEAGUES FROM DIFFERENT DEPARTMENTS OR TEAMS?

ANSWER: I collaborated with colleagues from different departments on a cross-functional project. I organized regular meetings, encouraged open communication, and ensured that everyone's expertise was leveraged effectively. This collaborative effort resulted in a seamless project execution.

67. DESCRIBE A SITUATION WHERE YOU HAD TO INNOVATE OR COME UP WITH A CREATIVE SOLUTION TO A PROBLEM.

ANSWER: In a previous role, we faced budget constraints for a marketing campaign. I proposed a creative and cost-effective digital marketing strategy that not only stayed within budget but also exceeded the campaign's objectives, showcasing innovation in problem-solving.

68. HOW DID YOU APPROACH THE CONVERSATION?

ANSWER: I provided constructive feedback to a colleague by focusing on specific behaviors rather than personal traits. I began with positive aspects, addressed the specific issue objectively, and suggested actionable improvements. This approach fostered a constructive dialogue and positive change.

69. Can You Share An Example Of A PROJECT WHERE YOU HAD TO MULTITASK AND MANAGE COMPETING PRIORITIES?

ANSWER: I managed competing priorities in a project by creating a detailed project plan, setting clear priorities, and regularly reassessing tasks. Efficient time management, delegation, and effective communication ensured successful project completion without compromising quality.

70. HOW DID YOU RESOLVE THE ISSUE AND MAINTAIN A POSITIVE RELATIONSHIP?

ANSWER: I addressed a dissatisfied customer by actively listening to their concerns, empathizing with their experience, and proposing a solution that exceeded their expectations. Timely follow-ups and continued engagement helped rebuild trust and maintain a positive relationship.

71. HOW DID YOU ENSURE A SMOOTH TRANSITION?

ANSWER: I led a team through a restructuring process by communicating transparently, addressing concerns, and providing support. I emphasized the positive aspects of the change, encouraged team collaboration, and ensured everyone felt heard and valued during the transition.

72. CAN YOU SHARE AN EXAMPLE OF A TIME WHEN YOU HAD TO INFLUENCE OR PERSUADE OTHERS TO ADOPT YOUR IDEA OR APPROACH?

ANSWER: I successfully influenced my team to adopt a new project management tool by highlighting its benefits, conducting training sessions, and showcasing improved efficiency and collaboration. Clear communication and demonstrating positive outcomes were key to gaining buy-in.

73. DESCRIBE A SITUATION WHERE YOU HAD TO HANDLE A MISTAKE OR FAILURE. HOW DID YOU TAKE RESPONSIBILITY AND LEARN FROM THE EXPERIENCE?

ANSWER: I took responsibility for a project setback by conducting a thorough analysis of what went wrong. I identified areas for improvement, implemented corrective measures, and shared the lessons learned with the team. This experience contributed to my continuous growth and improved decision-making.

74. TELL ME ABOUT A TIME WHEN YOU HAD TO DELEGATE TASKS TO TEAM MEMBERS. HOW DID YOU ENSURE ACCOUNTABILITY AND SUCCESSFUL COMPLETION OF THE DELEGATED WORK?

ANSWER: I delegated tasks by clearly defining expectations.

75. WHAT MOTIVATES YOU TO EXCEL IN YOUR WORK?

ANSWER: "I am motivated by the opportunity to contribute meaningfully to projects. I find fulfillment in overcoming challenges and continuously improving my skills."

76. DESCRIBE A SITUATION WHERE YOU TOOK INITIATIVE TO SOLVE A PROBLEM AT WORK.

ANSWER: "I noticed an efficiency gap in our processes and proposed a solution that streamlined operations, resulting in a 20% increase in productivity."

77. HOW DO YOU HANDLE SETBACKS AND FAILURES IN THE WORKPLACE?

ANSWER: "I view setbacks as opportunities to learn. I analyze the situation, identify areas for improvement, and apply those lessons to future projects."

78. DESCRIBE YOUR WORK STYLE IN THREE WORDS.

ANSWER: "Efficient, collaborative, and results-driven."

79. HOW DO YOU HANDLE FEEDBACK, AND WHAT STEPS DO YOU TAKE TO IMPROVE BASED ON IT?

ANSWER: "I appreciate constructive feedback as it provides valuable insights. I take the time to reflect on the feedback, identify areas for improvement, and implement changes accordingly."

80. WHAT STRATEGIES DO YOU USE TO MAINTAIN A POSITIVE ATTITUDE DURING CHALLENGING SITUATIONS?

ANSWER: "Recognizing a need for additional training, I proactively enrolled in relevant courses, enhancing my skills and bringing added value to the team."

81. WHAT DO YOU BELIEVE IS THE MOST IMPORTANT QUALITY IN A SUCCESSFUL TEAM?

ANSWER: "Open communication is crucial. A successful team thrives on transparency, mutual respect, and the ability to collaborate effectively."

82. WHAT STRATEGIES DO YOU USE TO STAY MOTIVATED DURING REPETITIVE OR MUNDANE TASKS?

ANSWER: "I find ways to add variety or challenge to the tasks, such as setting personal performance goals or finding innovative solutions to improve efficiency. Recognizing the importance of the task also helps maintain motivation."

83. WHAT ARE YOUR SHORT-TERM CAREER GOALS?

ANSWER: My short-term goal is to gain valuable experience in my field and develop specific skills that will contribute to my professional growth.

84. HOW DO YOU SEE YOUR
    CAREER PROGRESSING IN THE
    NEXT 2-3 YEARS?

ANSWER: In the next 2-3 years, I aim to take on more responsibilities, possibly move into a leadership role, and enhance my expertise in [specific area].

85. CAN YOU SHARE A SPECIFIC
    ACCOMPLISHMENT THAT
    ALIGNS WITH YOUR CAREER
    GOALS?

ANSWER: One of my notable achievements was [describe accomplishment], which showcased my ability to [relevant skill] and contributed to my career goals in [specific way].

86. WHAT STEPS ARE YOU TAKING
    TO IMPROVE YOUR SKILLS IN
    [SPECIFIC AREA]?

ANSWER: I am currently enrolled in a [relevant course/certification], and I consistently practice and apply these skills in my current role.

87. HOW DO YOU HANDLE SETBACKS IN YOUR CAREER, AND WHAT HAVE YOU LEARNED FROM THEM?

ANSWER: I view setbacks as opportunities to learn and grow. I analyze the situation, identify areas for improvement, and use the experience to enhance my skills and resilience.

88. WHAT MOTIVATES YOU TO ACHIEVE YOUR CAREER GOALS?

ANSWER: My motivation comes from the desire to make a meaningful impact in my field, continually challenge myself, and contribute to the success of the projects I'm involved in.

89. HOW DO YOU DEFINE SUCCESS IN YOUR CAREER?

ANSWER: Success, to me, is achieving a balance between personal satisfaction, professional growth, and making a positive impact on the team and organization.

90. WHAT ROLE DO MENTORSHIP AND GUIDANCE PLAY IN YOUR CAREER DEVELOPMENT?

ANSWER: I value mentorship as a crucial aspect of my career growth. Having a mentor provides guidance, insights, and a roadmap for achieving my career goals.

91. WHAT SPECIFIC STEPS ARE YOU TAKING TO ENHANCE YOUR LEADERSHIP SKILLS?

ANSWER: I am actively seeking leadership opportunities within projects, attending leadership development programs, and studying successful leaders in my industry.

92. HOW DO YOU ADAPT YOUR CAREER GOALS TO CHANGING INDUSTRY TRENDS?

ANSWER: I regularly assess industry trends, identify emerging opportunities, and adjust my career goals to align with the evolving needs of the industry.

93. CAN YOU DISCUSS A TIME WHEN YOU HAD TO REALIGN YOUR CAREER GOALS DUE TO EXTERNAL FACTORS?

ANSWER: During [specific situation], I had to reassess my goals. I adapted by acquiring new skills and redirecting my focus to align with the changing demands of the industry.

94. WHAT STRATEGIES DO YOU EMPLOY TO MAINTAIN A

HEALTHY WORK-LIFE BALANCE
WHILE PURSUING YOUR
CAREER GOALS?

ANSWER: I prioritize tasks, set realistic deadlines, and make time for activities outside of work that contribute to my well-being and personal development.

95. HOW DO YOU ENSURE THAT YOUR GOALS ALIGN WITH THE MISSION AND VALUES OF THE ORGANIZATION?

ANSWER: I align my goals with the organization's mission by understanding its values and incorporating them into my professional objectives. This ensures a cohesive approach to achieving both personal and organizational success.

96. WHAT STEPS ARE YOU TAKING TO BUILD A STRONG PROFESSIONAL NETWORK?

ANSWER: I actively participate in industry events, join professional associations, and connect with colleagues on platforms like LinkedIn to build a diverse and valuable network.

97. IN WHAT WAYS DO YOU SEEK FEEDBACK TO IMPROVE YOUR PERFORMANCE AND ACHIEVE YOUR GOALS?

ANSWER: I regularly seek constructive feedback from colleagues, supervisors, and mentors. This helps me identify areas for improvement and refine my approach to achieving my goals.

98. HOW DO YOU PRIORITIZE COMPETING CAREER GOALS WHEN FACED WITH MULTIPLE OPPORTUNITIES?

ANSWER: I prioritize goals based on their alignment with my long-term vision and the potential impact on my overall career. I weigh the pros and cons, considering both short-term and long-term benefits.

99. WHAT ROLE DOES CONTINUOUS LEARNING PLAY IN YOUR CAREER DEVELOPMENT?

ANSWER: Continuous learning is integral to my career development. I actively seek opportunities to expand my knowledge, stay informed about industry advancements, and adapt to changing trends.

100. HOW DO YOU PLAN TO LEVERAGE YOUR STRENGTHS TO ACHIEVE YOUR CAREER GOALS?

ANSWER: I leverage my strengths by identifying opportunities that align with them and by consistently applying these strengths to contribute meaningfully to projects and initiatives.

101. CAN YOU DISCUSS A TIME WHEN YOU HAD TO OVERCOME A SIGNIFICANT CHALLENGE IN YOUR CAREER PATH?

ANSWER: During [specific challenge], I overcame adversity by [describing actions taken]. This experience strengthened my resilience and determination to achieve my career goals.

102. CAN YOU SHARE AN EXAMPLE OF WHEN YOU HAD TO PIVOT YOUR CAREER STRATEGY TO SEIZE A UNIQUE OPPORTUNITY?

ANSWER: When presented with the opportunity to [specific opportunity], I pivoted my strategy by [describe actions taken]. This decision significantly contributed to my professional growth.

103. WHAT ROLE DOES MENTORSHIP AND GUIDANCE

PLAY IN YOUR CAREER
DEVELOPMENT?

ANSWER: Mentorship is invaluable to me.
I actively seek guidance from mentors who
provide insights, share experiences, and
offer advice that accelerates my career
development.

104. HOW DO YOU ENSURE THAT
YOUR CAREER GOALS ALIGN
WITH THE EVOLVING NEEDS OF
THE INDUSTRY?

ANSWER: I stay informed about industry
trends through continuous research,
networking with professionals, and
participating in relevant forums. This allows
me to adjust my goals to meet the changing
demands of the industry.

105. WHAT STEPS ARE YOU
TAKING TO MAINTAIN A
POSITIVE AND PROACTIVE

ATTITUDE IN PURSUING YOUR
CAREER GOALS?

ANSWER: I maintain a positive attitude by focusing on solutions rather than problems, setting realistic expectations, and celebrating small achievements along the way.

106. HOW DO YOU ENVISION YOUR ROLE CONTRIBUTING TO THE OVERALL SUCCESS OF THE ORGANIZATION IN THE LONG TERM?

ANSWER: In the long term, I see my role as contributing to

107. WHAT ATTRACTED YOU TO THIS POSITION?

ANSWER: Highlight aspects of the job that align with your skills, career goals, and passion for the industry.

108. HOW DID YOU HEAR ABOUT THE POSITION?

ANSWER: Be honest about the source, whether it was through a job board, networking, or a company employee.

109. WHY DID YOU RESIGN FROM YOUR PREVIOUS JOB?

ANSWER: Focus on seeking new challenges, professional growth, or a better alignment with your skills and values.

110. CAN YOU WALK ME THROUGH YOUR RESUME?

ANSWER: Provide a chronological overview of your career, emphasizing relevant skills and achievements.

111. WHAT EXPERIENCE DO YOU HAVE IN THIS INDUSTRY/ROLE?

ANSWER: Discuss specific projects, accomplishments, and responsibilities that showcase your expertise.

112.   DESCRIBE A CHALLENGING PROJECT YOU WORKED ON. HOW DID YOU HANDLE IT?

ANSWER: Detail the project, the challenges faced, and the steps you took to overcome them, emphasizing problem-solving skills.

113.   WHAT RELEVANT SKILLS DO YOU BRING TO THIS POSITION?

ANSWER: Align your skills with the job requirements, providing examples of how you've applied them in the past.

114.   DESCRIBE A SITUATION WHERE YOU HAD TO ADAPT TO UNEXPECTED CHANGES.

ANSWER: Illustrate your flexibility, problem-solving abilities, and how you successfully adapted to the changes.

115. TELL ME ABOUT A TIME YOU HAD TO COLLABORATE WITH A DIFFICULT TEAM MEMBER.

ANSWER: Discuss the challenges, your communication strategies, and the ultimate resolution or positive outcome.

116. WHAT MOTIVATES YOU IN YOUR WORK?

ANSWER: Talk about personal and professional motivations, such as achieving goals, continuous learning, or making a positive impact.

117. CAN YOU SHARE AN EXAMPLE OF A GOAL YOU SET AND HOW YOU ACHIEVED IT?

ANSWER: Discuss a specific, measurable goal, the steps you took to achieve it, and the positive results.

118. HOW DO YOU HANDLE CONSTRUCTIVE CRITICISM FROM YOUR TEAM MEMBERS?

ANSWER: Express openness to feedback, detail an example of receiving and implementing feedback, and highlight personal growth.

119. DESCRIBE YOUR PREFERRED WORK ENVIRONMENT AND MANAGEMENT STYLE.

ANSWER: Discuss the type of work culture where you thrive and your compatibility with various management styles.

120. WHERE DO YOU SEE YOURSELF IN FIVE YEARS?

ANSWER: Align your future goals with the potential career path within the company, showcasing your ambition and commitment.

121. WHAT ATTRACTED YOU TO THIS INDUSTRY, AND HOW DO YOU PLAN TO GROW WITHIN IT?

ANSWER: Discuss your passion for the industry, long-term aspirations, and how you plan to stay relevant and contribute.

122. HOW DO YOU HANDLE FAILURE OR SETBACKS IN YOUR CAREER?

ANSWER: Show resilience by discussing how you've turned setbacks into learning opportunities and improved your approach.

123. WHAT PROFESSIONAL DEVELOPMENT OPPORTUNITIES DO YOU ACTIVELY PURSUE?

ANSWER: Discuss conferences, workshops, certifications, or any ongoing education that enhances your skills and knowledge.

124. HOW DO YOU ENSURE WORK-LIFE BALANCE IN A DEMANDING ROLE?

ANSWER: Highlight your time management skills, boundaries, and strategies to maintain a healthy work-life balance.

125. CAN YOU GIVE AN EXAMPLE OF A SUCCESSFUL TEAM PROJECT YOU'VE WORKED ON?

ANSWER: Detail your role, collaboration with team members, and the positive outcome or impact of the project.

126. HOW DO YOU CONTRIBUTE TO A POSITIVE TEAM CULTURE?

ANSWER: Emphasize your communication skills, willingness to help others, and ability to foster a collaborative and supportive environment.

127. HOW DO YOU HANDLE WORKING WITH DIVERSE PERSONALITIES AND PERSPECTIVES?

ANSWER: Emphasize your adaptability, open-mindedness, and ability to appreciate and leverage diverse strengths within a team.

128. HOW DO YOU DEFINE TEAMWORK?

ANSWER: Teamwork is the collaborative effort of a group to achieve a common goal by leveraging each member's strengths and skills.

129. DESCRIBE A SITUATION WHERE YOU HAD TO WORK

CLOSELY WITH A TEAM TO
ACHIEVE A CHALLENGING
GOAL.

ANSWER: In my previous role, we had a
tight deadline for a project. I collaborated
with team members, dividing tasks based on
individual strengths, ensuring we met the
deadline successfully.

130. DESCRIBE A SITUATION
WHERE YOU HAD TO MOTIVATE
YOUR TEAM DURING A
CHALLENGING TIME.

ANSWER: In a tight deadline situation, I
motivated the team by highlighting the
importance of our work, acknowledging
their efforts, and offering support. This
helped boost morale and maintain focus.

131. HOW DO YOU HANDLE A
TEAM MEMBER WHO IS NOT
CONTRIBUTING THEIR FAIR
SHARE?

ANSWER: I would address the issue privately, understanding their perspective, and provide support if needed. If the problem persists, I would involve higher management to find a resolution.

132. CAN YOU SHARE AN EXAMPLE OF WHEN YOU HAD TO ADAPT YOUR COMMUNICATION STYLE TO EFFECTIVELY WORK WITH A DIVERSE TEAM?

ANSWER: In a multicultural team, I adapted my communication style by being mindful of cultural differences, using clear and concise language, and ensuring everyone felt comfortable expressing their thoughts.

133. DESCRIBE A SUCCESSFUL PROJECT THAT REQUIRED COLLABORATION WITH

INDIVIDUALS FROM DIFFERENT
DEPARTMENTS.

ANSWER: I collaborated on a
cross-functional project where I actively
engaged with members from various
departments, ensuring a holistic approach
that contributed to the project's overall
success.

134. HOW DO YOU HANDLE
CONFLICTING PRIORITIES
WITHIN A TEAM?

ANSWER: I would prioritize tasks based on
urgency and impact, communicate openly
with the team about the challenges, and
work collaboratively to find solutions or
adjustments to deadlines.

135. PROVIDE AN EXAMPLE OF
WHEN YOU TOOK THE
INITIATIVE TO SUPPORT A TEAM

MEMBER STRUGGLING WITH
THEIR TASKS.

ANSWER: Recognizing a team member's
struggle, I proactively offered assistance,
shared resources, and provided guidance,
ensuring they felt supported and ultimately
contributing to the team's success.

136. HOW DO YOU ENSURE THAT
ALL TEAM MEMBERS FEEL
HEARD AND VALUED DURING
MEETINGS?

ANSWER: I encourage active participation,
listen attentively to each team member, and
consider diverse perspectives.
Acknowledging contributions fosters a sense
of value and inclusivity.

137. DESCRIBE A TIME WHEN
YOU HAD TO COMPROMISE FOR
THE BENEFIT OF THE TEAM.

ANSWER: In a disagreement about project direction, I compromised by incorporating elements from both sides. This ensured a balanced approach and maintained a positive team dynamic.

138. HOW DO YOU BUILD TRUST WITHIN A TEAM?

ANSWER: Trust is built through transparency, consistency, and delivering on commitments. I ensure open communication and demonstrate reliability to foster a trusting team environment.

139. SHARE AN EXAMPLE OF WHEN YOU SUCCESSFULLY FACILITATED A BRAINSTORMING SESSION WITHIN YOUR TEAM.

ANSWER: I facilitated a brainstorming session by creating an open and non-judgmental environment, encouraging all team members to share ideas. We then collectively evaluated and refined the concepts.

140. HOW DO YOU HANDLE A SITUATION WHERE A TEAM MEMBER IS RESISTANT TO CHANGE?

ANSWER: I would empathize with their concerns, communicate the benefits of the change, and involve them in the decision-making process. Addressing their apprehensions helps ease the transition.

141. DESCRIBE A PROJECT WHERE YOU HAD TO COLLABORATE WITH REMOTE TEAM MEMBERS. HOW DID YOU OVERCOME COMMUNICATION CHALLENGES?

ANSWER: I utilized video conferencing tools, maintained regular updates through email and collaboration platforms, and

scheduled virtual meetings to ensure
seamless communication and coordination.

142. HOW DO YOU CELEBRATE TEAM SUCCESSES?

ANSWER: I celebrate team successes by
acknowledging individual contributions,
organizing team events, and expressing
gratitude. This fosters a positive team
culture and motivates everyone.

143. SHARE AN EXAMPLE OF WHEN YOU HAD TO MEDIATE A CONFLICT BETWEEN TWO TEAM MEMBERS.

ANSWER: I mediated a conflict by listening
to both perspectives, facilitating a
constructive conversation, and guiding them
to find common ground. Resolving the issue
strengthened their working relationship.

144. HOW DO YOU ENSURE THAT TEAM GOALS ALIGN WITH THE

OVERALL OBJECTIVES OF THE
ORGANIZATION?

ANSWER: I regularly communicate
organizational goals to the team, ensuring
that our projects and tasks align with the
broader mission. This helps everyone
understand their contribution to the bigger
picture.

145. DESCRIBE A TIME WHEN
YOU HAD TO STEP INTO A
LEADERSHIP ROLE WITHIN A
TEAM TEMPORARILY.

ANSWER: In the absence of our team
leader, I stepped up by coordinating tasks,
maintaining communication, and ensuring
everyone stayed focused on our goals. This
experience strengthened my leadership
skills.

146. HOW DO YOU HANDLE A
SITUATION WHERE A TEAM

MEMBER IS NOT OPEN TO
FEEDBACK?

ANSWER: I approach the situation
delicately, focusing on constructive
feedback and emphasizing its positive
impact on personal and team growth.
Building a culture that values feedback helps
overcome resistance.

147. SHARE AN EXAMPLE OF
WHEN YOU HAD TO MANAGE
CONFLICTING PRIORITIES
WITHIN YOUR TEAM.

ANSWER: I managed conflicting priorities
by involving the team in priority-setting
discussions, ensuring alignment with
organizational goals, and making
adjustments based on workload and
deadlines.

148. HOW DO YOU PROMOTE A
COLLABORATIVE CULTURE IN A
TEAM?

ANSWER: I promote a collaborative culture by encouraging open communication, recognizing and rewarding collaboration, and fostering an environment where team members feel comfortable sharing ideas and opinions.

149. DESCRIBE A SITUATION WHERE YOU HAD TO HANDLE A TIGHT DEADLINE. HOW DID THE TEAM COLLABORATE TO MEET IT?

ANSWER: Facing a tight deadline, I organized a quick team meeting to strategize, redistributed tasks based on individual strengths, and ensured constant communication to meet the deadline successfully.

150. HOW DO YOU HANDLE A SITUATION WHERE A TEAM MEMBER IS CONSISTENTLY UNDERPERFORMING?

ANSWER: I address the issue by providing constructive feedback, offering support, and setting clear expectations. If the problem persists, I work with the individual to create a performance improvement plan.

151. DESCRIBE A PROJECT WHERE YOU HAD TO WORK WITH A DIVERSE TEAM WITH VARYING SKILL SETS.

ANSWER: I collaborated on a diverse team with members having different skills. By understanding each team member's strengths, we allocated tasks accordingly, ensuring a balanced and successful project outcome.

152. HOW HAVE YOU BEEN ENCOURAGING CREATIVITY AND INNOVATION WITHIN YOUR TEAM?

ANSWER: I encourage creativity by fostering an environment where team members feel comfortable expressing their ideas

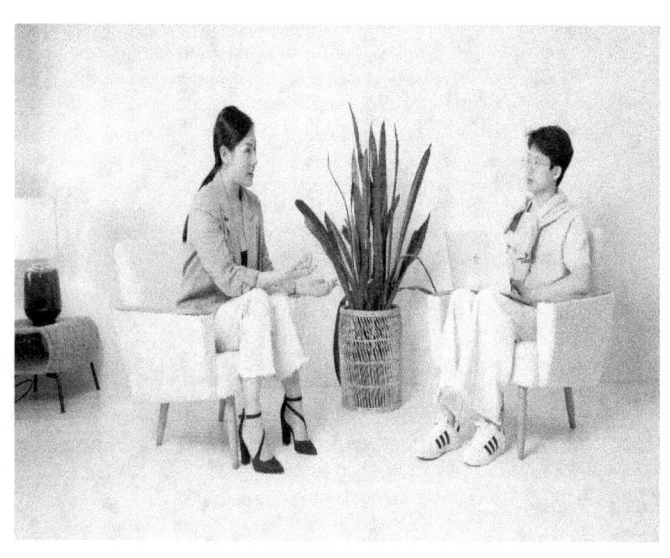

CHAPTER SIX

UNDERSTANDING THE INTERVIEWER'S CONCERNS

Job interviews serve as critical junctures in the professional journey, where candidates vie for opportunities and employers seek the right fit for their teams. Amidst the exchange of resumes and qualifications, an often underestimated aspect comes to the forefront – understanding the interviewer's concerns. These concerns, though implicit, significantly influence the outcome of the interview and can be deciphered through careful observation and preparation.

Interviewers are tasked with evaluating not just the technical prowess of candidates, but also their interpersonal skills and cultural alignment with the organization.

One common concern is whether the candidate possesses the right blend of hard and soft skills. Job descriptions usually outline the technical requirements, but interpersonal dynamics are equally pivotal. an astute candidate recognizes this and tailors responses to demonstrate both technical proficiency and an ability to collaborate and adapt to the organization's culture.

Moreso, interviewers often harbor concerns regarding a candidate's commitment to the role and the company. frequent job changes on a resume might raise eyebrows, signaling potential instability. An effective strategy involves addressing this concern proactively, showcasing how each career move contributed to skill development and aligning with the current role's requirements.

A well-crafted narrative can help dispel doubts about a candidate's long-term commitment.

Another dimension of concern centers around a candidate's adaptability and resilience. industries are evolving at an unprecedented pace, and employers seek individuals who can navigate change with composure. interviewers might pose scenario-based questions or inquire about past experiences that required adaptability. successful candidates not only narrate instances where they embraced change but also highlight the skills acquired during such transitions.

Understanding the concerns of interviewers also involves decoding non-verbal cues. interviewers may display subtle signs of skepticism or interest through body language, tone, or facial expressions. an attentive candidate picks up on these cues, adjusting their approach accordingly. If an interviewer seems skeptical, addressing concerns directly and providing concrete examples can instill confidence.

Furthermore, interviewers often evaluate a candidate's alignment with the organization's values and mission. a misalignment on these fronts can be a deal-breaker. To assuage these concerns, candidates should delve into the company's ethos beforehand and articulate how their personal values align with the organizational culture.

Demonstrating a genuine connection to the company's mission not only addresses concerns but also sets the candidate apart as someone genuinely invested in the company's success.

The interviewer's concern about a candidate's future potential plays a pivotal role. employers are not just hiring for the current role but envisioning the candidate's growth within the organization.

Addressing this concern involves discussing aspirations, showcasing a commitment to continuous learning, and exemplifying how one's skills can contribute to the company's future endeavors.

A successful job interview requires more than a recitation of qualifications; it demands an acute understanding of the interviewer's concerns. Candidates who delve into the implicit worries of the interviewer, showcasing a blend of technical expertise, adaptability, commitment, and cultural alignment, stand a better chance of leaving a lasting impression.

By decoding verbal and non-verbal cues, addressing concerns proactively, and weaving a narrative that aligns with the organization's values, candidates can navigate the interview dynamic with finesse, securing not just a job but a meaningful professional partnership.

CHAPTER SEVEN

CONCLUSION

In the dynamic realm of professional growth, mastering the art of answering interview questions is an indispensable skill. As we navigate the labyrinth of interviews, it becomes evident that success hinges not just on eloquence but on a strategic blend of research, effective communication, and adept question-handling.

Research, the unsung hero of interview preparation, unveils the company's ethos and current industry trends. Armed with this knowledge, candidates transcend the ordinary, crafting responses that resonate with the organization's core values. A well-researched interviewee isn't just a candidate; they're a potential collaborator who understands the nuances of the company culture.

Effective communication during an interview is the linchpin that transforms information into impact. It's not merely about conveying facts; it's about connecting on a human level. The subtle dance of verbal and non-verbal cues, coupled with active listening, paints a vivid portrait of a candidate who not only speaks but comprehends, resonating with interviewers at a visceral level.

Navigating the interview landscape is akin to a well-choreographed dance, and knowing the steps is crucial. Begin with a confident entrance, showcasing your enthusiasm. As the rhythm of questions unfolds, maintain eye contact and exude positivity. Be articulate, concise, and illustrative in your responses, transforming potential stumbling blocks into stepping stones toward success.

Cracking the code of interview questions involves more than rehearsed responses; it's about showcasing authenticity while aligning personal experiences with the role's demands. Embrace the STAR method – Situation, Task, Action, Result – to structure your answers, weaving a compelling narrative that leaves a lasting impression.

The interview arena is where preparation meets opportunity. Research, effective communication, and adept question-handling create a symphony that resonates with interviewers, elevating you from a mere candidate to the candidate. As you step into the spotlight, armed with insights and finesse, remember: the interview isn't just a Q&A; it's your moment to shine, to captivate, and to carve your path to success.

LETTER TO MY READERS

Dear Beloved Readers,

I am filled with gratitude and warmth as I extend my sincerest thanks to each and every one of you who chose to embark on the journey of exploring the pages of my book, "Interview Questions and Answers." Your decision to delve into the insights and knowledge shared within its chapters means the world to me.

Writing this book was a labor of love, fueled by the passion to provide you with valuable information, guidance, and perhaps a new perspective on the intricacies of interviews. Knowing that you've taken the time to read it is not only humbling but also incredibly motivating.

In a world abundant with choices, I am honored that you selected my work to accompany you on your quest for knowledge and self-improvement. Your support is the driving force behind every word penned, and your engagement with the material makes the entire process immensely rewarding.

As you navigate the pages, I hope you find the answers you seek and gain insights that prove instrumental in your personal and professional endeavors. Your feedback, thoughts, and reflections on the book are always welcome, and I look forward to continuing this enriching dialogue.

Once again, thank you for choosing "Interview Questions and Answers." May it serve you well on your journey, and may the knowledge within its pages empower you in all your future interviews and pursuits.

With heartfelt appreciation,

Dora Harris

www.ingramcontent.com/pod-product-compliance
Lightning Source LLC
Chambersburg PA
CBHW062335290526
45794CB00005B/2037